A gift for

_____

From

_____

There has only been one Christmas—

the rest are anniversaries.

—W. J. CAMERON

A KEEPSAKE CHRISTMAS

ALICE GRAY *and* SUSAN WALES

COUNTRYMAN

Project manager—Terri Gibbs

Published in association with Loyal Arts Literary Agency, www.loyalarts.com.

Photo credits: Chris Garborg
Corel Photos, pages 5, 20, 24, 49
Digital Vision, pages 1, 6, 8, 11, 19, 40, 44, 45, 51, 58, 61, 65, 72, 83, 88, 95, 96
iStockphoto, pages 35, 38, 52, 67, 92, 97, 110
Janis Christie/Photodisc Green/Getty Images, page 80

Designed by Garborg Design Works, Savage, Minnesota.

ISBN: 1-4041-0218-3

www.thomasnelson.com
www.jcountryman.com

Printed and bound in the United States of America

Contents

*The heart is like a treasure chest
that's filled with souvenirs;
it's where we keep the memories
we've gathered through the years.*

—UNKNOWN

PREFACE

Twinkling lights drape across the mantel, a cozy fire crackles on the hearth, we turn a page on the calendar—and Christmas is here once more. This is the wondrous season when ordinary moments become extraordinary and when greetings of "welcome home" moisten our cheeks with joyful tears. It's a time for reflecting on the cherished blessings of Christmases past—and a time for dreaming new dreams.

This book is written especially for every woman who longs to create a meaningful and memorable Christmas. As you turn the pages, you'll find wonderful new ideas, inspirational stories, delicious recipes, easy decorating tips, suggestions for stress-free entertaining, and tender ways to connect with others. Best of all, there is a golden thread lacing through all the pages—the timeless message that Christmas was a birthday before it was a holiday.

As you celebrate this wondrous season, our prayer is that it will truly be a Christmas to remember—a treasured keepsake of the heart.

Alice and Susan

Welcoming CHRISTMAS

Welcome to my heart

Spirit of Christmas

I've been waiting for you . . .

all year!

—KIMBER ANNE ENGSTROM

Celebrating Advent

Celebrating Advent is a wonderful way to welcome Christmas into your heart and home!

An advent wreath is traditionally made of evergreens symbolizing God's eternal love. Four candles—three purple and one pink—are arranged around the wreath at equal points. A white candle is placed in the center. Each candle has a special significance and is lighted at specific times.

Beginning with the fourth Sunday before Christmas, some families gather for activities every night and others just on Sundays. Older children often enjoy leading devotions and lighting the candles; even the youngest child can help by extinguishing them. Singing Christmas carols, praying together, and reading Bible passages will make your Advent celebration even more meaningful.

10

WEEK ONE—*The Candle of Hope* represents the promise of a Savior. Read Isaiah 9:6–7 before lighting one purple candle for hope.

WEEK TWO—*The Candle of Peace* is for the Prince of Peace, Jesus Christ. Read about His birthplace in Micah 5:2 and Luke 2:1–5 before lighting two purple candles for hope and peace.

WEEK THREE—*The Candle of Joy* is for the tidings of great joy the angels announced to the shepherds. Read Luke 2:8–14 before lighting three purple candles for hope, peace, and joy.

WEEK FOUR—*The Candle of Love* represents God's love for the world when He gave His only Son. Read John 3:16 and Luke 2:15–20 before lighting three purple candles for hope, peace, and joy—and the pink candle for love.

CHRISTMAS EVE—*The White Christmas Candle* celebrates Jesus Christ as the Light of the World. Read Isaiah 9:2 and John 8:12 before lighting all five candles.

Break off a branch of a cherry tree at the beginning of Advent. Keep it in water in a warm room and the flowers should burst into bloom at Christmastime.

God grant you:

The light in Christmas, which is faith.

The warmth of Christmas, which is love.

The radiance of Christmas, which is purity.

The belief in Christmas, which is truth.

The all of Christmas, which is Christ.

—WILDA ENGLISH

Different Ways to Count the Days

~ Make a green and red paper chain with twenty-five loops. Write different names of family members and friends on each loop. Cut off one loop each night and pray together as a family for the person whose name is on the loop.

~ Help your child write out twenty-five kind deeds on slips of paper: call Grandmother, give mommy three hugs, draw a picture for a neighbor. Tape each slip of paper to a simple gift like a hair clip or piece of candy. Put them all in a Christmas stocking and have the child draw one each day—doing the kindness as well as receiving the gift.

> Today's Christmas should mean creating happy hours for tomorrow and reliving those of yesterday.
> —*Gladys Taber*

~ Set up a little Christmas tree in a child's room. Each day open a tiny box and pull out a miniature ornament to decorate the tree. The tradition can be repeated each year using the same ornaments.

~ Purchase an Advent calendar kit and fill it with little gifts or Bible verses for the children to enjoy each day of Advent.

Yule Log Festivities

Burning a Yule log is among the oldest Christmas Eve traditions. Like the candles on the advent wreath, its flame represents the light that Jesus brought into the world.

Yule log celebrations can be quite elaborate or very simple. The customary tradition begins near dusk on Christmas Eve when families tramp through the woods to find a suitable log and then drag it home amidst much singing and laughter.

Before the log is ignited, it is saturated with fragrant spices and children distribute sprigs of holly tied with bright ribbons to each guest. Once the fire is ablaze, the holly sprigs are tossed into the flames symbolizing that the wrongs of the past are forgiven and forgotten.

Keeping the Yule log tradition can be as simple as rubbing a log with fragrant spices, setting it on a bed of dried holly leaves, and igniting it on Christmas Eve. Some families fashion table centerpieces from small logs embellished with candles and holly; and some prefer serving a cake-roll filled with coffee flavored butter cream, iced with chocolate, and decorated with holly leaf candies.

Whether simple or elaborate, the Yule log tradition is a fun way of welcoming Christmas.

~ Heavenly scents for your fireplace: Fill a twelve-inch square of tulle or fine netting with a cup each of lemon and orange peels. Add four crushed cinnamon sticks and the gratings of two whole nutmegs to the citrus peels. Sprinkle these ingredients with four drops of cinnamon or pine essential oils. Tie the bundle with a red or green ribbon and toss the fragrant bundle into the fire along with a few pine branches for a divine Christmas fragrance that will waft throughout your home. These heavenly scents make great gifts for friends and neighbors, too.

~ Activity for children: Purchase a jellyroll cake from the bakery. Provide the children with a can of frosting, a plastic knife, and some small Christmas candies. Let them frost and decorate their own miniature Yule log.

~ In place of the traditional Advent wreath, design a small Yule log to hold the five-advent candles. Embellished with holly and greenery, it can double as a pretty table centerpiece.

It isn't the holly, it isn't the snow.

It isn't the tree, nor the firelight's glow.

It's the warmth that comes to the hearts of men

When the Christmas spirit returns again.

—UNKNOWN

Candle of Hope

By JOHN FISCHER
AUTHOR AND SONGWRITER

When my children were younger, we developed an unusual family tradition. Since we lived only two blocks from church, we always walked to and from the Christmas Eve service. The cold night air, the Christmas lights, and the possibility of snow all added to the festivity of the evening.

The church service always ended with a candle-lighting ceremony accompanied by the singing of "Silent Night." For this, each person received a small hand-held candle. The church was darkened and the pastor would light his candle from the Christmas candle in the center of the Advent wreath. Then the pastor would light one candle on the front row, and soon the whole room would be glowing as the flame was passed from person to person.

This is where our own family tradition took over. We didn't blow out our candles at the end of the service as everyone else did. We figured that if the light had lasted that long, we wanted to keep our candles burning all the way home to light our Yule log, which was waiting in the fireplace.

One year the wind was so cold and strong that we had to huddle tightly together to keep our candles from going out—slowly inching our way against the storm, lighting and relighting from whoever kept their flame burning.

From Advent candle to living room fire—from spiritual fire to home fire burning—this light represented Christmas hope. It is a memory I'll always cherish.

Then Jesus spoke to them again, saying,
"I am the light of the world.
He who follows Me shall not walk in darkness,
but have the light of life."

John 8:12
New King James Version

The Candy Maker's Story

White candy canes have been used to decorate Christmas trees for centuries, but it was not until the early 1900's that red stripes were added. The charming story of how a candy maker used the candy cane to symbolize Christ's love is a sweet way to remind your children of the true meaning of Christmas.

~ The white part of the candy represents the purity of Jesus.

~ The red stripes remind us of Christ's death on the cross.

~ The crook at the top looks like a shepherd's staff and helps us remember that shepherds were the first to hear about the Savior's birth.

~ Turned upside down, the candy cane looks like the letter J, symbolizing the first letter in Jesus' name.

CANDY CANE BARK

1 pound of white or dark chocolate morsels
   or squares
$^1/_2$ cup peppermint candy canes, crushed

Melt the chocolate in a double boiler over medium heat, stirring constantly until smooth or melt it in a microwave at thirty-second intervals, stirring the chocolate between each interval. Add the crushed candy canes to the melted chocolate mixture and stir until the peppermint pieces are evenly distributed. Cover a cookie sheet with waxed paper and pour the chocolate mixture onto the cookie sheet and spread with the back of a wooden spoon. Freeze the candy for one hour or until it hardens, then peel the waxed paper off and break the candy into bite-size pieces.

～ Print the symbolism of the candy cane on small cards. Hole punch the cards and thread red ribbon through them to tie the cards to some candy canes. Arrange the candy in a little basket for guests or let your children give them to friends, neighbors, or residents of a nursing home.

～ For a festive flower vase, glue candy canes around the outside of a coffee can.

～ Tie ribbon around a napkin and tuck a candy cane in the loop of the ribbon for a holiday napkin ring.

～ Core half a dozen apples and insert candy canes in the center of the apples. Group the apples around a pillar candle, and accent with greenery for a novel centerpiece.

Spreading
THE JOY

*Keeping Christmas
is good, but sharing
it is better.*

—ARNOLD GLASS

Let us remember that the

Christmas heart is a giving heart,

a wide open heart that

thinks of others first.

—GEORGE MATTHEW ADAMS

Opening Your Heart and Your Home

> Somehow, not only for Christmas,
> But all the long year through,
> The joy that you give to others,
> Is the joy that comes back to you.
> —*John Greenleaf Whittier*

The holidays have arrived! Amidst all the hustle and bustle of the season, don't you feel a longing to create special memories with friends and family? Your home is aglow with twinkling lights and candles, holiday music fills the air, and a pot of wassail simmers on the stove—its fragrance wafting through the house. There are special touches everywhere to greet guests who knock at your beautifully wreathed door. Ah, Christmas—it's the perfect time to open wide the doors of your heart and home.

A Christmas Tea Party

Christmas is such a splendid time for celebrating friendships. What better way to celebrate than to gather mothers, daughters, grandmothers, and friends for an afternoon tea? This is a special time for little girls to bring along their favorite doll or teddy bear. And what girl, young or old, doesn't love to dress up? Light scented candles, play soft Christmas music in the background, and sip tea while you savor sweet memories.

> Come and share
> a pot of tea,
> My home is warm and
> my friendship's free.
> —Emilie Barnes

One of the advantages of a Christmas tea party is that your home already looks festive with holiday trim. Here are a few added touches that will make your tea all the more memorable:

～ For a centerpiece, fill a teapot with red or white roses mixed with evergreen sprigs and accented with gold ribbon. Scatter rose petals around the teapot.

～ Fill a sugar bowl with sugared rose petals to sweeten the tea. (See how to create the rose petals on page 28.)

~ Set the table with your best silver, china, and linens.

~ Arrange cookies, teacakes, candies, and scones with curd or jam, and tea sandwiches on the table.

~ To delight your young guests, set a small table with a miniature tea set for the children's dolls and teddy bears. Place a rosebud in a teacup for a centerpiece.

Offer a variety of teas and coffee to your guests. For a special treat sprinkle a tablespoon of cinnamon in your coffee before brewing. Be sure to have plenty of hot chocolate for the younger guests and garnish their mugs with a stick of peppermint that will slowly dissolve into the chocolate.

Before your guests arrive, create simple party favors by tucking tea bags and a few recipes for the goodies that were served at the tea inside Christmas cards. Arrange the cards in a pretty basket or bowl for your guests to pick up as they depart.

Make this special tea party an annual tradition for celebrating Christmas love with friends and family.

SUGARED ROSE PETALS

2 dozen fresh rose petals, washed
1 cup pre-packaged pasteurized egg whites
1/2 cup granulated sugar
Small paintbrush

Beat the egg whites in a bowl until frothy. With a fine brush, carefully apply a thin coat of the egg whites to both sides of each petal. Sprinkle the petal evenly with granulated sugar. Gently shake off any excess sugar and place the petal on a cake rack or waxed paper to dry overnight. Arrange the petals in a sugar bowl and serve with silver tongs to sweeten and float in tea. The petals can also be arranged upon cakes and cookies for edible decoration.

CHRISTMAS TEA SANDWICHES

2 loaves of sliced white bread
1 cup Craisins®
2 pounds prepared chicken salad
1 cup chopped pecans

Cut slices of the bread with cookie cutters in the shape of a holiday star, bell, or tree. Mix the Craisins® and pecans into the chicken salad. Spread the mixture onto the bread shapes and serve open face.
Yield—48 tea sandwiches.

Progressive Mug Party

A delightful way to celebrate the holidays with your neighbors is to organize a Progressive Mug Party. Each person brings a favorite Christmas mug and prizes are awarded for the biggest, prettiest, the funniest, and the most unusual.

At the first house appetizers are served and the partygoers' mugs are filled with a choice of eggnog, wassail, or hot chocolate. The second stop is for salad. A hearty soup entrée and baskets of crusty French bread await the hungry guests at the third home. Last of all this yummy dessert is served:

Place a brownie in the bottom of each mug. Next add a scoop of peppermint ice cream, drizzle with chocolate syrup and top with a dollop of whipped cream.

End the evening with a round of Christmas carols—and to all a good night!

> There's more, much more, to Christmas
> Than candlelight and cheer;
> It's the spirit of sweet friendship
> That brightens all year.
> —*Unknown*

29

TASTY BAKED POTATO SOUP

4 large baked potatoes, cooled, peeled, and cubed
12 strips bacon, cooked and diced
   (save 2 slices for garnish)
2/3 cup butter
1 8-ounce carton sour cream
2/3 cup all purpose flour
1-1/2 cups cheese, shredded
7 cups milk
1 teaspoon salt
4 onions, thinly sliced
1 teaspoon pepper
Garnish for each bowl of soup:
Crumbled bacon, grated cheese, and freshly
   chopped chives

Melt the butter in a large Dutch oven over low heat. Add the flour, stirring until smooth. Gradually add the milk and stir until the sauce thickens. Raise the heat slightly and add the potatoes and onions. Stir until the mixture begins to bubble. Lower the heat and add the sour cream, cheese, salt, and pepper. Stir continuously until the cheese is melted. Pour hot soup into individual bowls and sprinkle with the above garnishes. Serve immediately.
Serves—6–8.

WORLD'S YUMMIEST EGGNOG

2 quarts of eggnog
Whipped cream
1/2 gallon of vanilla ice cream
Nutmeg

Just prior to serving, mix the eggnog and ice cream in a blender or pour these ingredients into a bowl and blend them with a mixer. When blended the mixture should have the consistency of a milkshake. Pour it into Christmas mugs, add a dollop of whipped cream, and sprinkle with nutmeg, and garnish with a cinnamon sick. Yield—one gallon.

A Cup of Christmas Cheer

WASSAIL

- 1 tablespoon whole cloves
- 1 quart orange juice
- 6 cinnamon sticks
- 1 quart pineapple juice
- 3 tablespoons crystallized ginger
- 2 cups lemon juice
- 3 3/4 cups white sugar
- 1 gallon apple cider
- 2 quarts of water
- 6 lemon and orange slices
- 2 additional tablespoons whole cloves

Wrap the cloves, cinnamon sticks, and ginger in a six-inch square of cheesecloth and tie with a string. In a medium saucepan, combine the spice bag with the sugar and water. Simmer and stir this mixture until the sugar dissolves. Remove the sugar water with the spice bag from the heat and refrigerate overnight. Transfer the sugar water and the spice bag into a large pot and add the juices and the cider. Heat the mixture over a medium flame, being careful not to let it boil. Remove and discard the spice bag and pour the wassail into a punch bowl. Stud the orange and lemon slices with whole cloves and float them in the bowl of wassail. Serve warm. Yield—2 gallons.

Here we come a-wassailing
Love and joy come to you,
And to you your wassail, too,
And God bless you,
and send you a Happy New Year.

—"Here We Come A-Wassailing"

31

It only takes a spark to get a fire going,

And soon all those around

Can warm up to its glowing

That's how it is with God's love

Once you experience it

You spread His love to everyone

You want to pass it on!

—KURT KAISE

Fa, la, la, la, la, la, la, la—la!

> Caroling, caroling
> thru the town
> Christmas bells
> are ringing
> —*Wilha Hudson*

Organizing a caroling party is a fun way to share the joy of Christmas. Distribute copies of the music when the carolers gather at your home for a quick cup of wassail. Go caroling through the neighborhood, hospitals, nursing homes, or homeless shelters. After an evening of song, return home for Christmas cookies and coffee or hot chocolate.

~ Nursing homes: Pass out pretty Christmas cards. Make certain you have enough for every resident.

~ Hospital: Take a basket filled with sprigs of holly tied with red bows and ask the nurses to distribute them to patients who have no flowers or Christmas décor.

~ Children's wing: Take a basket of books with selections for various ages.

~ Homeless shelter: Ask each caroler to purchase several pair of warm socks, mittens, hats, or scarves to distribute at the shelter.

Especially at Christmas

By CELESTINE SIBLEY
From CHRISTMAS IN GEORGIA

Things aren't important, people are, Muv preached, and it sounded so fine it was years before I realized what she meant to us. Things weren't important to us, so as fast as gift packages came in from distant kin, Muv unwrapped them, and with a gleam in her eye that I came to dread said happily, "Now who can we give this to?"

It's funny that with the passage of the years only one or two of the things stand out in memory. There were some lavender garters a boy in the sixth grade gave me. "Beautiful!" said Muv. "You can give them to Aunt Sister!" And there was a green crepe de chine dress I think I still mourn for a little bit. "Oh, it's so pretty! Don't you want to give it to Julia Belle?"

Julia Belle was a skinny little girl in the quarters who had lost her baby in a fire and kept wandering up and down the road wringing her hands and crying. My green dress was such a dazzling gift, it did divert her from her grief a little, and it may have helped her along the road to recovery.

At the time I remember protesting that I loved the dress and wanted it myself and Muv said blithely, "Of course you do. It's no gift if it's something you don't care about!"

It must be true because the other Things are lost to memory, but the People remain. Through the years there have been a lot of them, disreputable, distinguished, outrageous, inspiring, and at Christmastime I remember them and the gifts they gave to me—the gifts in fact, that they were.

Christmas is most truly Christmas when we celebrate it

by giving the light of love to those who need it most.

—RUTH CARTER STAPLETON

Christmas Movie Night

> "Look, Daddy, teacher says,
> 'every time a bell rings,
> an angel gets his wings.'"
> —*It's A Wonderful Life*

Cards to write, cookies to bake, presents to wrap; the list is endless— sometimes it seems like there's no time to relax with friends. The perfect solution is to host a movie night. Invite your guests to wear their sweats or pajamas and robes with comfy slippers. Provide pillows for everyone and serve something simple like apples, popcorn balls and cookies. Catch the holiday spirit while watching your favorite Christmas movie.

OLD FASHIONED POPCORN BALLS

8 cups of popped corn
1/2 teaspoon salt
1/2 cup dark corn syrup
1/2 cup brown sugar
1/3 cup water
1 teaspoon vanilla
1/2 cup margarine or butter
1 cup peanuts

Mix together the corn syrup, water, butter, salt, and sugar in a heavy saucepan. Place the pan over medium heat stirring constantly until the mixture comes to a boil. Remove the pan from the heat and stir in the vanilla and peanuts. Pour the hot syrup over the popcorn a little at a time, stirring constantly until all of the popcorn is coated. Let the popcorn cool until it becomes easy to handle. Grease your hands with butter and form the popcorn into balls. Yield—6–8 servings.

SNOWBALLS

2 tablespoons butter or margarine
1/2 cup powdered milk
3 tablespoons water
3 cups coconut flakes
1 teaspoon vanilla
6 ounces chocolate morsels

Melt the butter in a microwave oven or over low heat, and add the water and vanilla. In a separate bowl add the sugar and powdered milk. Gradually add these ingredients to the butter mixture and mix well. Stir in the coconut and drop by teaspoonfuls onto the waxed paper. Let the balls stand until firm. Melt the chocolate morsels and swirl over each ball. Store in the refrigerator. Yield—3 dozen.

Christmas Morning

Oh, the excitement of Christmas morning! The family gathers round the tree, ribbons are snapped, packages unwrapped, and the children squeal with delight. Christmas is finally here! Make the morning extra special by serving an easy-to-prepare brunch for everyone to enjoy as they celebrate this blessed day.

SAUSAGE RING

2 pounds sausage
1/2 cup milk
1 cup apples, chopped
1 1/2 cups cracker crumbs
1/2 cup onions, minced
1 16 ounce can of apricots
2 eggs, beaten
1/2 cup pecans, toasted
Fresh parsley

Note: This dish can be prepared one day in advance.

Sauté the sausage in a skillet and add the apples and onions. Cook the mixture until the vegetables are tender. Drain off the excess liquid and add the eggs, milk, and cracker crumbs. Pour the sausage mixture into a ring pan that has been lightly sprayed with cooking oil, cover with foil and refrigerate overnight. The next morning preheat the oven to 350 degrees. Bake the ring for approximately thirty minutes or until it sets. Turn the sausage ring out onto a heated platter. Fill the apricot halves with toasted pecans and arrange the fruit around the sausage ring. Garnish the platter with parsley. For a special treat, you can also fill the center of the ring with scrambled eggs topped with grated sharp cheddar cheese. Delicious! Serves—8-12.

EGGNOG FRENCH TOAST

2 eggs
1/8 teaspoon cinnamon
1/2 cup eggnog
2 tablespoons butter
1/8 teaspoon nutmeg
4 slices of cinnamon raisin bread

Beat the eggs and eggnog together. Add the nutmeg and cinnamon. Soak each slice of bread in the egg mixture until it is coated and set it aside. Melt the butter in a skillet. Add the bread, and heat until each piece is golden. Flip the bread over and repeat with the other side. Serves—4.

LAURA BUSH'S

HOT CHOCOLATE

6 tablespoons unsweetened cocoa
6 teaspoons sugar
Pinch of salt
2 1/2 cups of milk
2 1/2 cups light cream
1/2 teaspoon or more vanilla
Pinch of cinnamon
Whipped cream
Orange zest

Mix the cocoa, salt, and sugar. Add this mixture
to the milk and heat until it dissolves. Add the
light cream, cinnamon, and vanilla to the milk
mixture and heat to just under boiling. Stir the
mixture well and pour into warm mugs. Top
with whipped cream, cocoa powder, and a fine
orange zest. Serves—4–6.

No Peeking!

◇ After everyone's gone to bed on Christmas Eve, Father ties a wide red ribbon across the bottom of the staircase. On Christmas morning, no one dares sneak past the ribbon until Father ceremoniously cuts it and lets everyone run to the tree.

—THE JOE HUEY FAMILY

◇ When the children wake up on Christmas morning they burst into their grandparent's room to wake up Grandfather. Dressed in his red flannel nightshirt, Grandfather Rush, the a descendant of a signer of the Declaration of Independence, leads our family in a favorite carol as we wind down the stairs to the Christmas tree to open gifts.

—ACTRESS SARAH RUSH

◇ Christmas morning our family travels from house to house for a progressive brunch. At each stop we exchange presents and enjoy the food and fellowship.

—KIMBERLY MORRISSEY

◇ Can't go home for the holidays? We make a home movie—singing carols and giving personal greetings— and send it to our family to watch on Christmas morning. It's the next best thing to being there.

—VICKIE FOARD

◇ Unlike when they were younger, the girls now sleep late. They're not the ones waking us up—we make hot chocolate and wake *them* up!

—FIRST LADY LAURA BUSH

Keeping CHRISTMAS

May we keep Christmas
in our hearts,
that we may be kept
in its hope.

—PETER MARSHALL

Christmas is the season of love,

a time for gathering together

and celebrating the

greatest gift of all

—the arrival of the Savior.

—ANONYMOUS

46

Cherished Traditions

For all of us,
today's experiences
are tomorrow's
memories.

—*Barbara Johnson*

There's something quite wonderful about taking a wistful journey to Christmas past, where the memories of time-honored traditions linger like the fragrance of scented candles: children's faces pressed against frosty windows as they wait for Grandpa and Grandma to visit, father reading the Christmas story from the worn pages of his Bible, hands clasped in blessing around a bountiful table.

As women, we long to create precious traditions that will be passed on to future generations. And intuitively we know the most treasured traditions will be those that focus on family, friendship, peace, hope, and love. Sprinkled through the next few pages is a potpourri of simple ideas to help you create the meaningful memories you desire. Surely the most cherished will be those that keep Jesus as the center of your Christmas celebrations.

The Real Treasure

By JUDY GORDON

Ann smiled with anticipation as she unwrapped her most cherished Christmas decoration—an exquisite, hand-painted nativity scene. Piece by piece, the white tissue paper fell away, revealing the noble wise men, the handsome Joseph, and the delicate face of Mary. The soft pastels and artistic detail filled Ann with pleasure as she marveled again at her good fortune in finding this unique and beautiful set.

Years ago in a shop full of hodgepodge, Ann had discovered the dusty box on a low shelf—a hidden treasure until uncovered by her exploring. From her first glimpse, she knew it would always be her favorite Christmas decoration.

Anne cleared off the mahogany sideboard and placed each figure in or near the crèche before unwrapping the one she always saved for last—baby Jesus. Carefully removing the paper, Ann couldn't believe what she saw. The cherubic figure of Jesus had shattered into pieces—too many to even think about gluing back together. Not only was the nativity piece broken. So was Ann's heart.

Finding a duplicate figure would be impossible, but maybe she could at least come close. Phone book in hand, Ann was perched at the breakfast bar listing gift shops when she heard her son, Bobby, come bounding in from school. A silent pause preceded his burst into the kitchen. His brown eyes wide with six-year-old wonder, he cried, "Mom, baby Jesus is missing! We can't have Christmas without Jesus."

Ann's pen stopped midstroke as Bobby's words pierced her heart. She had been so distraught over her broken nativity that she was missing a greater treasure. Christmas is much more than presents and decorations—more than a painted figure in a manger. Much more, indeed.

The meaning behind Bobby's words flickered for a moment like a forgotten candle and then brightened to shine like the Christmas star. It's true, Ann thought. Jesus is the treasure, and we can't have Christmas if we're missing Him.

Happy Birthday, Jesus!

Wouldn't it be wonderful if every home could have a birthday cake for Jesus? Before your family opens their presents, light the birthday candles, hold hands, and sing "Happy Birthday" to Jesus. The youngest person to the oldest will be reminded that Christmas was a birthday before it was a holiday.

CAKE DECORATING

～ Let the children help to decorate the cake.

～ Use a single candle to represent Jesus as the Light of the World—or twenty candles representing the centuries since His birth.

～ White frosting represents the purity of Christ.

～ Use red trim as a symbol of the Lord's death and green as a symbol of new life in Christ.

～ A gold star will remind everyone of the Christmas star that appeared in the sky the night Jesus was born.

～ If you don't have time to bake and decorate, you might want to order your cake from the bakery. How fun to watch the clerk's eyes light up when you ask to have a cake decorated with the words, "Happy Birthday, Jesus."

TREASURE HUNT

Before your guests arrive, hide the nativity pieces. If necessary, add extra angels, sheep, or shepherds so each person can find one item. Once the pieces are found, read the Christmas story from Luke 2:1–20 and Matthew 2:9–11. As each nativity piece is mentioned in the Bible story, ask the person holding the figure to place it around the manger. Let the children have fun. It's quite wonderful if a child snuggles a sheep next to Jesus in the manger.

FOLLOW THE STAR

Depending on the weather, this game can be played inside or outside. At nightfall, select a leader and give that person a powerful flashlight. Everyone—even grandma and grandpa—lines up behind the leader. Turn on the flashlight and switch off all the other lights. Shine the flashlight on the ceiling or treetops and follow the leader through the house, garage, and yard. The journey ends at the crèche. Read the Christmas story and sing, "O Little Town of Bethlehem."

On Bended Knee

O little town of Bethlehem,
how still we see thee lie!
Above thy deep and
dreamless sleep
the silent stars go by.
—*Phillips Brooks*

Even today, you can see sheep grazing contentedly in the rocky fields just outside Bethlehem. Not far from what is known as the Shepherd's Fields is the Church of the Nativity—the oldest church in the Holy Land and, it is believed, the very place where Jesus was born on that angel-announced night so long ago.

The door to the church is small and narrow, the lintel so low that all must stoop to enter. It seems very fitting that to visit the birthplace of the King of kings, one must enter on bended knee.

The hinge of history is on the door of a Bethlehem stable.
—*Ralph W. Stockman*

CHRISTMAS PAGEANT

Gather a selection of clothes and props and give children—and adults, if you need a larger cast or just want to include everyone—a few minutes to dress for the Christmas pageant. Once they are ready, the narrator reads the Christmas story from the Bible. Members of the cast enter and take their places as the story unfolds.

Props can include silver garland to circle the heads of angels, bathrobes for shepherds, a loose dress for Mary so a baby doll can fit discreetly beneath it, a basket and cloths for when the baby is "born," paper crowns or shimmering yardage remnants for the Magi, odds and ends for the Magi's gifts. Stuffed teddy bears, dogs, and lambs can fill in for the animals—or younger children can play the parts in masks and footed pajamas. The more props you have, the more fun the costumes. Even a net petticoat from a castoff square-dancing outfit can be transformed into wonderful angel wings.

Take pictures, laugh wonderfully at the costumes, and share the incredible joy of celebrating the birth of Christ.

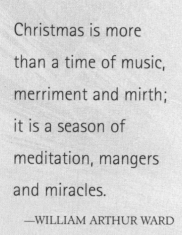

Christmas is more than a time of music, merriment and mirth; it is a season of meditation, mangers and miracles.

—WILLIAM ARTHUR WARD

MANGER HAYSTACKS

(A favorite of the Billy Graham family.)

1 3-ounce package cream cheese, room temperature
2 tablespoons milk
3 cups confectioner's sugar
1 1-ounce square unsweetened chocolate, melted
1/4 teaspoon vanilla
1/2 cup chopped nuts
Dash of salt
3 cups small marshmallows
Flaked coconut

Combine the softened cream cheese and milk and mix well. Gradually add the sugar. Stir in the melted chocolate, vanilla, nuts, and salt, then fold in the marshmallows. Drop rounded teaspoons of the mixture into the coconut and toss until well covered. Chill until set. Yield—2 dozen cookies.

God walked down the stairs of heaven with a Baby in His arms.

—*Paul Scherer*

After Christmas dinner, we always videotape the children's nativity play and talent show. Next we have a birthday party for Jesus with balloons and a cake that reads, Happy Birthday, Jesus.

—THELMA WELLS, WOMEN OF FAITH

~

After Christmas, we'll store the tree under the porch until the Friday before Easter when we'll take the barren tree and fashion it into a cross. On Easter morning, our family will decorate it again, this time with flowers and colorful eggs symbolizing new life in the resurrected Lord.

—PASTOR DAVID AND KRISTIE STRODER

~

After setting up the crèche, we put the wise men in another part of the house and each night we move them a little closer to the manger.

—NANCY LARSON, GRANDMOTHER

Christmas may be a day of feasting, or of prayer, but always it will be a day of remembrance— a day in which we think of everything we have ever loved.

—AUGUSTA E. RUNDEL

55

Mary's Song

—LUCI SHAW

Blue homespun and the bend of my breast

keep warm this small hot naked star

fallen to my arms. (Rest...you who have had so far to come.)

Now nearness satisfies

the body of God sweetly. Quiet he lies

whose vigor hurled

a universe. He sleeps

whose eyelids have not closed before.

His breath (so slight it seems

no breath at all) once ruffled the dark deeps

to sprout a world.

Charmed by dove's voices, the whisper of straw,

he dreams,

hearing no music from his other spheres.

Breath, mouth, ears, eyes
he is curtailed
who overflowed all skies,
all years.
Older than eternity, now he
is new. Now native to earth as I am, nailed
to my poor planet, caught that I might be free,
blind in my womb to know my darkness ended
brought to this birth
for me to be new-born,
and for him to see me mended
I must see him torn.

Giving GIFTS

May you have the
greatest two gifts of
all on these holidays:
someone to love and
someone who loves you.

—JOHN SINOR

The Art of Giving

"The Gift of the Magi," first published in 1906, is a touching tale of newlyweds too poor to buy Christmas gifts. Ultimately each sacrifices his or her dearest possession to buy a present for the other. The message of O. Henry's classic story is still true today: gifts given from the heart are the ones we treasure most.

> The magi, as you know, were wise men—wonderfully wise men—who brought gifts to the Babe in the manger. They invented the art of giving Christmas presents.
> —O. Henry,
> FROM "THE GIFT OF THE MAGI"

Meaningful gifts can be as simple as time spent with a lonely neighbor, a love note on your husband's pillow, a whispered prayer—everyday gifts that keep the spirit of Christmas all year long.

True giving knows no season.
—Florence E. King

Peace on earth will come to stay
when we live Christmas every day.

—*Helen Steineer Rice*

EVERYDAY GIFTS OF THE HEART

FOR HUSBANDS—

Bake his favorite dessert

Show respect

Pray for him daily

Take interest in his work

Let go of past disappointments

FOR YOUNG CHILDREN—

Frame their art pieces

Talk and pray at bedtime

Tuck love notes in a lunchbox

Swing together in the park

Volunteer in their classroom

FOR TEENS—

Listen without interruption

Help their dreams come true

Eat meals together

Write notes of encouragement

Attend their activities

FOR FRIENDS—

Walk together in the rain

Forgive an oversight

Pray for their families

Keep their confidences

Celebrate their successes

Hailey's Gift

By MEGAN CHRANE

We never should have waited so long to shop for presents, but there we were in the crowded mall three days before Christmas. Spotting an empty bench, my grandmother, Mimi, offered to watch my two-year-old daughter Hailey while I dashed into a candle shop for one last gift.

Hailey had just settled herself on the bench when she called out to a passerby, "Merry Christmas." Without responding, the elderly woman clutched her soiled brown paper bag a little closer and kept walking. Undaunted, Hailey repeated her cheery greeting: "Merry Christmas." A moment later, in spite of Mimi's attempt to restrain the exuberant toddler, Hailey scampered down from the bench and lifted up her pudgy little arms to the startled woman.

Now, turning toward Mimi, the stranger timidly asked, "Is it okay for me to hold the little girl?" Mimi was unsure, but after catching the pleading look in the woman's eyes, she smiled warmly and nodded yes.

The tattered hem of the stranger's dark blue coat formed a circle around her as she painstakingly knelt down on one knee and opened her arms. Unhesitatingly, Hailey snuggled close, laying her head on the woman's shoulder. With silent tears settling in the creases of her face, the stranger gently rocked back and forth as though keeping time with a distant lullaby.

"The baby sure likes you," Mimi said. "You must be a very special grandmother."

Before she could answer, Hailey reached up her tiny hand and softly patted the lady's cheek.

Huskily, as though still choking back tears, the stranger replied, "No, I never got to be a grandmother." Then, with the sadness lifting for a moment, she smiled. "But today God gave me a gift I've always longed for—to hold a baby in my arms."

. . .

When I rushed back from the candle shop with the last present, Mimi was holding Hailey on her lap. Tears glistened beneath Grandmother Mimi's lashes as she told me about their encounter with their elderly friend. I surveyed all the bundles and packages surrounding me and realized they were only trinkets. God had already given us the real gifts—a baby born in a manger long ago, and today, a babe held in a stranger's arms.

Gift-Giving Traditions

> It's not how much
> we give
> but how much love
> we put into giving.
> —*Mother Teresa*

∼ Our Christmas gifts for the grandchildren are always wonderful books. After writing personal notes inside the covers, we tie a festive ribbon around a stack for each grandchild. No matter what their ages, the books are among their favorite gifts.

—DEE BOLEN
retired school teacher

∼ One thing we have always done is to keep the kids' presents to three. Three presents just like the baby Jesus got from the wise men.

—KATHIE LEE GIFFORD,
television personality

∼ At our holiday table, each family member shares a Christmas memory. Our stories span five generations and as the stories unfold, they weave a rich tapestry of family heritage.

—ARTHUR JOSEPH HUEY
great grandfather

∼ My grandparents always have a brightly wrapped package under the tree with "Jesus" written on the tag. The box has a slit in the top and everyone secretively puts money in it to donate to a charitable organization or needy family.

—BREANAH GRAY
teen

One year my mother asked us to think of a gift we would like to wrap up and place under the tree for Jesus. These gifts were the first we opened on Christmas morning. My dad's gift was his planner to symbolize that he wanted his time to belong to God. Mine was a collage made from magazine scraps to represent important things in my life—meaning I wanted every area of my life to be Christ-like.

Although we did our "tradition" only once, it shaped my thinking about the real meaning of giving gifts at Christmas.

—DANAE JACOBSON
university student

On our first Christmas Eve together, my husband Richard surprised me with an unexpected present. Inside the beautiful wrappings was an Easy Bake Oven—a toy I had always wanted as a child but one my parents were unable to afford. As I marveled over my childhood dream come true, Richard said, "Unless you still want to bake a cake, why don't we take this over to the Children's Hospital tonight and make some little girl very happy?" Thus began our annual tradition of buying toys for needy children instead of presents for one another at Christmastime.

—LAURA BURKETT JACOBSON
film producer

A Christmas Carol

—CHRISTINA GEORGINA ROSSETTI

What can I give Him,

Poor as I am?

If I were a shepherd

I would bring a lamb,

If I were a wise man

I would do my part,

Yet what can I give Him,

Give my heart.

Easy to Make—Lovely to Give

Instead of a hectic day shopping at the mall, invite a friend over to share in a bit of homespun charm. Turn on some Christmas music, sip a cup of tea, laugh and share dreams as you work together making wonderful and unique gifts.

ROSEBUD POMANDER

You'll want to make several of these fragrant pomanders—they are wonderfully elegant for every woman and easy enough for children to make.

3-inch Styrofoam ball
Essential oil of rose
White glue
6 ounces of dried miniature rosebuds

Cover the top half of the foam ball with glue. Completely cover the top half of ball with rosebuds. Let it dry and repeat with the lower half of the ball. Sprinkle essential oil of rose over the ball and spray with hairspray to fix. For a variation, you can use miniature pinecones sprinkled with drops of essential oil of pine.

The best of all gifts around any Christmas tree;
the presence of a happy family all wrapped up in one another.
—*Burton Hillis*

CHOCOLATE SPOONS

Chocolate spoons wrapped in cellophane and tied with a bow are perfect to accompany gifts of special-blend coffee or coffee mugs.

20–24 heavy plastic red, green, white, or silver spoons
6 ounces white chocolate
6 ounces dark chocolate
Red and green sugar, optional

Line two cookie sheets with waxed paper. Put the white and dark chocolate in separate bowls. Melt each chocolate in the microwave. Select one minute on high and stir the chocolate thoroughly at fifteen-second intervals until it is smooth. Dip the spoons in dark chocolate or white chocolate and drizzle with the contrasting color. For a holiday touch, you could also dip the chocolate spoons in green or red sugar. Arrange the spoons on cookie sheets with their handles propped on the side. Refrigerate until the chocolate hardens. Wrap the spoons in cellophane and tie with a ribbon.

FIRESIDE CAPPUCCINO

This spicy cappuccino is yummy on a chilly day. Imagine your friend settling deep in her favorite chair, snuggling into the warmth of a cozy throw, and sipping a cup of this fragrant brew.

1 cup powdered chocolate milk mix
1/2 to 1 cup sugar
3/4 cup instant coffee
1 teaspoon cinnamon
1 cup powdered non-dairy creamer
1/2 teaspoon ground nutmeg
1 tablespoon dried orange peel

Blend all the ingredients on high until well mixed in a blender. Pour the blended ingredients into a jar. Cover the jar lid with pretty fabric or wrap the jar in cellophane and tie with a ribbon. Add a tag or label that reads: Mix 2-3 teaspoons with a cup of hot water. Top with a dollop of whipped cream and stir with a chocolate spoon.

SIMMERING SCENTS

Your friends will love having this scent waft throughout their homes not only during the holidays but also all year long.

1/2 cup dried or fresh orange peel
6-inch square of tulle
2 cinnamon sticks, crushed
8 drops essential oil of orange
1 tablespoon whole cloves
Ribbon

Mix the orange peel, cinnamon, and cloves in a bowl to form the potpourri. Sprinkle the mixture with essential oil of orange. Pour the potpourri mixture into the tulle square and tie it with a ribbon. Attach a tag with these directions: Drop the bag into two quarts of water and simmer on the stove.

CHRISTMAS PECANS

4 cups pecan halves
3/4 cup sugar
2 egg whites
1 teaspoon salt
1 tablespoon of cold water
2 tablespoons pumpkin pie spice

Preheat your oven to 300 degrees. Beat the egg whites and water until fluffy. Add the pecans to the egg mixture. Toss to coat. In a separate bowl, combine the sugar, salt, and pumpkin pie spice. Toss the pecans in the sugar mixture until all the pecans are well coated. Spread the pecans in a single layer on a greased aluminum foil lined cookie sheet. Bake for 15–20 minutes until golden. Remove the pecans from the oven and spread on waxed paper to cool. Break up any clusters. Yield—4 cups.

EASY ENGLISH TOFFEE

2 sticks butter
1 cup sugar
1 6-ounce package of chocolate morsels
1 cup pecans, coarsely chopped

Line a 13 x 9 x 2-inch pan with waxed paper. Sprinkle the bottom of the pan with 1/3 cup of the pecans. Combine the butter and sugar in a saucepan over medium heat and stir with a wooden spoon until the liquid reaches the hard crack stage or 300 degrees on a candy thermometer. Pour the hot mixture over the pecans in the pan. Spread the chocolate morsels evenly over the pecan mixture. Sprinkle the remaining nuts over the morsels and press them into the mixture. Refrigerate the candy for two hours; then break into pieces. Yield—2 1/2 to 3 dozen pieces of candy.

I love receiving the gift that giving gives!

—KIMBER ANNE ENGSTROM

Bookmarks

Here's an easy yet elegant gift for your book-loving friends.

Choose a pretty velvet or tapestry ribbon that's at least an inch wide. Cut a ten-inch piece and trim the top with pinking shears so it won't ravel. Fold the other end into a point and tack it in place with a couple of stitches. Sew a bead or charm onto the end of the point to weight the bookmark and add a pretty touch.

> My first copies of *Treasure Island* and *Huckleberry Finn* still have some blue-spruce needles scattered in the pages. They smell of Christmas still.
> —*Charlton Heston*

ADDITIONAL GIFT IDEAS

∼ Using spray adhesive, glue sheets of silver leaf to small glass votive candleholders and brush off the excess silver.

∼ Decorate a recipe box and include some holiday family recipes.

∼ Buy a plain journal and add a few of your favorite Scriptures or quotes.

∼ Lightly spray terracotta pots with silver or gold paint and fill them with homemade cookies or other goodies. Wrap them in cellophane and tie with a ribbon.

∼ Tie a bunch of like candles together with a pretty silk Christmas ribbon.

∼ Dip pretzels in melted chocolate. While they are still warm, sprinkle them with crushed peppermint candies. Arrange the cooled pretzels in a glass container and wrap a festive ribbon around it.

∼ Trace your child's hand on construction paper, cut it out and glue it to felt backing. Glue a photo to center of hand. To use as an ornament, hole punch and add yarn for a tree hanger. This is a nice gift for children to make and give.

Summer's Tears

Giant tears slid down three-year old Summer Malu's rosy cheeks. Gathering her in my arms I asked, "What's the matter, sweetheart?"

"The p-p-picture. The one I made for you, Nana," she sobbed. "I forgot to bring it."

How very dear to be so concerned about a gift not given instead of a gift not received!

> A candle is a lovely thing;
> It makes no noise at all,
> But softly gives itself away,
> While quite unselfish, it grows small.
> —Eva K. Logue

It's a Wrap!

Invite a few friends over for a gift-wrapping party. Each guest brings her own wrapping supplies including gift tags, scissors, and tape. Like an old-fashioned quilting bee, the conversation is as valuable as the tasks your hands accomplish.

~ Remove the top of a Christmas ornament and place a gift of money or jewelry inside. At the top, tie a bow through the holder.

~ Adorn your packages with natural trims: pinecones, twigs, seashells, dried flowers, or cinnamon sticks.

~ Attach a candy cane, a snowman cookie, or a holiday lollipop for a sweet package.

~ Instead of gift tags, use a color copier to print a favorite photograph of the recipient and attach it to the package.

~ Use luggage tags for gift tags to add a useful gift.

~ Substitute pretty fabric for wrapping paper. Tie the package with tulle or netting.

~ Spray pressed leaves with gold or silver paint. Dry and affix them to packages with spray adhesive.

~ To wrap a DVD use an empty popcorn container from a theater and add a package of microwave popcorn.

~ Ha! Ha! For a relative with a sense of humor, or for children, a great gift-wrap is the comics section of the newspaper.

~ Let your child create an original holiday gift-wrap, using white paper, glitter, crayons, or stickers.

Party Gifts

Next time you're invited to a holiday party, offer to bring a cheese ring or strawberry tree—either one is heavenly.

CHEESE RING
—FIRST LADY ROSAYLYN CARTER

1 pound sharp Cheddar cheese, finely grated
1 cup mayonnaise
1/2 cup onion, chopped finely
1 cup pecans, chopped
Dash of cayenne pepper
6 twists black pepper, freshly ground
1-12 ounce jar strawberry preserves
Whole-grain crackers or Melba toast

Combine the cheese with the mayonnaise, chopped nuts, and onions. Mix in black pepper and cayenne pepper and blend thoroughly. Press the mixture into a three-cup ring mold. Refrigerate for at least two hours. To serve, dip the mold into a pan of hot water for 15 to 20 seconds before turning out onto a serving platter. Fill the center of the cheese ring with strawberry preserves and serve at once with whole-grain crackers or Melba toast. Serves—6–8.

STRAWBERRY TREE

Using cocktail toothpicks,
cover a Styrofoam cone with
lettuce and then attach
strawberries. Guests can take
a toothpick with a strawberry
and dip it in a side dish of
vanilla yogurt. For variety,
substitute tomatoes for the
strawberries and serve with
Ranch dressing.

Decking THE HALLS

Christmas waves a magic wand over this world, and behold, everything is softer and more beautiful.

—NORMAN VINCENT PEALE

Christmas!

No other time grants us, quite the vision—

round the tree or gathered before the fire,

we perceive anew with joy, one another's faces.

—ELIZABETH BOWEN

Holiday Ambience

Boughs of holly, beribboned wreaths, glowing candles, and gaily wrapped packages seem to fill every nook and cranny of the house. The lush evergreen tree is layered with glittering ornaments, a fire crackles, and seasonal fragrances mingle to form a scent best described as happiness. Is it any wonder that joyful laughter rings through the walls at Christmastime?

Christmas is not in tinsel and lights and outward show. The secret lies in an inner glow.

—Wilfred A. Peterson

Christmas—that magic blanket that wraps itself about us, that something so intangible that it is like a fragrance.

—August E. Rundel

Dazzling Decor

Even a few touches of holiday splendor can magically transform your home into a Christmas wonderland. Create the atmosphere you desire by choosing a few favorites from the following pages of easy decorating ideas.

SIMPLE CENTERPIECES

~ Wrap the bottom section of an 8-inch square box with beautiful paper. Place a small poinsettia plant in the box and trail ribbon down the sides. For a larger table, use three boxes and plants.

~ For a sparkling display, fill a grouping of champagne glasses with fresh cranberries and nestle a votive candle in each glass.

~ Arrange lemons, limes, oranges, pomegranates, or apples in a glass bowl and intersperse with sprigs of cedar or pine. To make your fruit glow, polish it with olive oil or dip it into a large bowl of liquid floor wax. The wax will help preserve the fruit.

~ Place three pillar candles of varying heights on a plate. Circle the candles with a garland of greenery and add sprigs of berries for a splash of color.

~ Arrange a collection of music boxes, snowmen, or figurines and flank the grouping with candles.

~ Fill a glass bowl with colored water, add your favorite essential oil of peppermint, and float candles in the water.

~ Tip the edges of tall pinecones with glue and dip them in glitter. Place the cones on a bed of greenery or angel hair sprinkled with confetti stars.

~ Position a pillar-candle inside a glass bowl, and then fill the bowl with cranberries or red and white striped peppermint candies.

~ Display a bowlful of colorful ornaments, gold-tipped pinecones, or oranges spiked with cloves and tied with ribbons.

TOPIARY TREES

A topiary centerpiece built with fruit lends fragrance and beauty to your holiday table. Set the arrangement on a bed of glossy evergreen leaves or place it in a flower pot. Choose lemons, limes, apples, crabapples, kumquats, tangerines or cranberries to create your tree. Design a grouping of fruit trees at varying sizes for a spectacular centerpiece. Swirl silk ribbons throughout the arrangement for drama.

Start with a cone of florist foam. Depending on the size of the fruit, use florist picks or toothpicks to attach the fruit to the cone. Continue adding fruit until the foam is completely covered. Tuck greenery sprigs or baby's breath into the spaces between the fruit.

SUGARED FRUIT

Frosty fruits arranged in a glass bowl make a dazzling centerpiece for the holidays. Mix evergreens in with the fruit and surround the bowl with candles to make your setting complete.

Fresh fruits
Superfine sugar
Pre-packaged pasteurized egg whites
Waxed paper
Large size re-sealable plastic bag

Pour the sugar into the plastic bag. Dip a paintbrush into the egg whites and paint the fruit sparingly with the egg whites. Place the fruit in the plastic bag and shake it gently until the fruit is covered with sugar. Shake off any excess sugar and place the fruit to dry on a rack for twenty-four hours. Carefully arrange the sugared fruit in a decorative glass bowl.

Something for the Children

Sometimes the very best memories are made when children climb up on a stool alongside mother to help in the kitchen—aprons hanging to their ankles, flour smudged on flushed cheeks, fingers in the frosting bowl, and smiles that go on forever.

Here's a recipe that is just perfect for memory-making.

> It is good to be children sometimes, and never better than at Christmas, when its mighty founder was a child Himself.
> —*Charles Dickens*

MINI-GINGERBREAD HOUSE

9 squares graham crackers
1/2 cup ready-to-spread white frosting
1 tube of decorator icing
Candy decorations: M & M's, gumdrops, candy canes,
    peppermint drops, and sprinkles.

For the floor of the house, place 1
cracker flat on a plate, and use 4
graham crackers for the walls,
gluing the seams with frosting. Cut 1 cracker in half
diagonally. Use the frosting
to attach the graham halves
to opposite ends of house to
form the roof supports. Attach
2 more crackers to form roof,
sealing all the edges with frosting. Allow one hour for the
frosting to dry. Cut the remaining grahams and attach as doors
and windows. Use the frosting
to coat one side of the house
and decorate it with candy.
After that side dries, frost the
opposite side and decorate it
with candy. Pipe on seams,
doors, and windows with decorator
frosting. Sprinkle powdered sugar on the plate
all around the house to create the effect of snow.

Garlands

Decorating with garlands is a wonderful way to cozy up your home and add a touch of old-fashion charm.

~ Take a trip to the woods to find boughs of pine and cedar or when selecting your Christmas tree, ask for extra greenery to use for decorating. Soak the greenery in water and keep it in a cool place until you are ready to use it.

~ For a full flowing garland, layer cedar and pine and secure with florist wire. Secure the garland in place with thin florist wire and tiny nails as you drape around stairways, windows, doorways, and mantels.

~ Embellish the garland by weaving red ribbon through the branches or by tying a large red bow at each end.

~ Add berry springs, dried or fresh fruit, or flowers in water tubes, gingerbread cookies, or twinkle lights to your garland.

~ Use garlands for hanging and displaying Christmas cards or photographs.

~ For a touch of nostalgia, make garlands out of popcorn, cranberries, kumquats, crab apples, or cinnamon sticks. String them together using a 1 1/2 -inch long needle threaded with dental floss.

~ Children can make pretty garlands by stringing together colored pasta and draping it on a Christmas tree.

~ Spray seashells, starfish or sand dollars with gold and silver spray paint. After the paint has dried, drill a small hole in the shells and string together with dental floss or floral wire.

A Light in the Window

Placing a candle in the window on Christmas Eve dates back to early Christianity. This charming tradition symbolized lighting the way for Mary and Joseph as they journeyed to Bethlehem. In Colonial times, window candles burned to welcome weary travelers needing a place of hospitality and comfort for the night. Some families with children in the military later adopted the tradition and kept a light shining continuously until their loved ones returned home.

Today a candle in the window at Christmastime shines brightly as a cheery welcome to your guests.

> Simple candles glowing in each window served as warm beacons to those approaching the household.
> —*Alda Ellis*

TRIM FOR WINDOWS AND DOORS

~ Place electric candles in your front windows to welcome guests.

~ Tack a long ribbon at the top of an interior window frame and let a small green wreath dangle from the ribbon.

~ Hang a harness of jingle bells over your front door handle to delight arriving guests.

~ Place a plastic vase inside a Christmas stocking and fill it with flowers or greenery and hang on a door.

~ Hang a wreath inside the front door as well as outside.

~ Frame your windows and doors with twinkling lights.

~ Assist your children in cutting out snowflakes to affix to the inside of the windows for a wintry look.

~ Use red ribbon to tie cellophane-wrapped peppermint candies to a wire wreath. Layer candy until the wreath is completely covered and hang the wreath on the inside of the front door. Dangle a pair of child's scissors from the wreath, and as your guest leave, invite them to cut a piece of candy off the wreath.

~ Cover your front door in a festive gift-wrap paper. Add a ribbon with a bow.

Oh Christmas Tree!

The Christmas tree—adorning shop windows, town squares, churches, and homes—has become one of the most beloved symbols of the holiday season. For many Christians, its evergreen branches symbolize the everlasting hope that Christ brought into the world.

The custom of using lights on the tree began in the sixteenth century and is credited to Martin Luther. One clear, cold December night, the story goes, Luther was walking home through the woods. Tired and discouraged from his journey, he rested for a moment in a grove of tall fir trees. As he gazed up through the trees at the starry sky, it looked to him as though thousands of stars had settled on the branches.

Moved by the illuminating beauty, Luther desired to recreate the effect for his children. Chopping down a small tree and taking it home, he fastened candles in metal holders to the evergreen branches. Placing glittering candles on the tree became a favorite tradition for the Luther family. Eventually, the idea spread around the world and, today, lights on the Christmas tree are among the best-loved decorations.

TIPS FOR SELECTING THE PERFECT TREE

∼ Before shopping for a tree, pre-measure the size of your tree stand and the space where you plan to put the tree.

∼ Take along a pair of gloves, a tape measure, and an old sheet or blanket to wrap around the tree to protect your car.

∼ Trees such as a Frazier or Noble Fir stay fresh longer. Their shorter needles make it easier for decorating, offer more space between branches, and provide stronger stems to hold heavier ornaments.

∼ The needles should look shiny, green, and fresh. Pull on the branch to test to see if any needles fall off or bend a branch to see if it snaps. Both of these indicate a tree that is not fresh.

∼ Spray the tree with insect repellent and place it in a bucket of water for at least twenty-four hours to refresh before placing in your home.

∼ Refill the tree stand with water daily.

As the lights of the Christmas tree
rose higher and higher,
she saw them now as stars in heaven.
—*Hans Christian Andersen*
"THE LITTLE MATCH GIRL"

The journey of my life can be traced through the Christmas ornaments my mother made for me, beginning the year I was born. From the blue ornament with iridescent stones that marked the year I got my first little pair of eyeglasses at age eight to the satin ball embellished with pearls and lace snipped from my wedding gown—each keepsake ornament provides a treasured memory. —NANCY STAFFORD, actress

~

Throughout our daughter's childhood we bought live Christmas trees and afterwards planted them in our backyard. Every year, we reminisce about Christmas Past as we drive through our old neighborhood and get a glimpse of "our" trees. —KEN WALES, film and television producer

He who has no
Christmas in his heart
will never find
Christmas under a tree.
—*Roy L. Smith*

Create a Critter Tree

This sweet custom of remembering the winter needs of birds and animals began in the thirteenth century. It is said that on Christmas morning, St. Francis of Assisi always provided extra corn and hay as a simple gesture to honor the animals that were in the stable when Jesus was born.

Whether out in the woods or in your own yard, decorating a critter tree with edible ornaments for God's small creatures can be a fun family tradition.

∽ Tie ears of dried corn, carrots, and oranges to the branches of trees or large shrubs.

∽ Spread peanut butter on bagel halves, sprinkle with birdseed, and hang on a tree.

∽ Make garlands with popcorn, berries, and mini-shredded wheat cereal to drape over tree branches.

∽ Core apples and fill them with peanut butter. Secure the apples to the trees with floral wire.

∽ Pack pinecones with ground suet or peanut butter mixed with raisins and berries, and hang from a ribbon on the tree.

For it is in giving that we receive.
—*St. Francis of Assisi*, PATRON SAINT OF ANIMALS

Add Sparkle to Your Porch and Yard

◇ Create a welcome path to your door with luminaries. Pour one cup of sand into the bottom of a small paper bag or quart size jar. Set a votive candle in the center of the sand and light before your guests arrive. Tip: Fold down two inches of the paper bag to make it sturdier.

◇ Add a string of battery-powered twinkling lights to your front door wreaths and garlands.

◇ Position a spotlight in your yard so it shines on a simple wooden manger. Use real hay under a baby doll wrapped in a blanket. Some families have a tradition of bringing the baby inside at nighttime if the weather gets especially cold.

◇ Fill grapevine balls with lights and dangle from the trees in your yard.

◇ Make a candle tree by placing votive candles in jelly jars, wrapping wire around the lips of the jar, and securing tightly to leafless trees.

◇ Arrange evergreen branches in flower pots. Decorate with twinkling lights and place at the corners of your front porch.

AND ALL AROUND THE HOUSE

~ Tie ribbons around your sofa pillows so they look like Christmas packages.

~ Dangle ornaments, candy canes, holly sprigs, mistletoe, or family photos from the arms of your chandelier.

~ Until Christmas Eve, tuck sprigs of evergreen and holly in Christmas stockings and hang on your mantel.

~ If you use place cards on your table, write verses from the Christmas story in Luke 21:1-20 on the back of the cards. Let your guests each read a verse before the blessing.

~ Decorate the refrigerator door with photos of past Christmas holidays. Everyone will enjoy reminiscing.

~ Delight your family by hanging an inexpensive plastic shower curtain in the bathroom and gluing decorations on it with a glue gun.

~ Preserve berries for decorations by dipping them in paraffin and letting them dry on a newspaper overnight.

~ Invite dinner guests to sign your linen tablecloth. Trace the handprints of younger children. Afterwards, embroider the names and handprints with red and green thread or a use a different color for each year. It will become one of your family's most cherished possessions.

Finding
ROOM

And she brought forth her firstborn Son,
and wrapped Him in swaddling cloths,
and laid Him in a manger,
because there was no room for them
in the inn.

—LUKE 2:7 New King James Version

We must always remember this—

Christ was created not as a season but as a gift.

This gift is for eternity

therefore Christmas always is.

—KIMBER ANNE ENGSTROM

Simplicity

Gingerbread houses, tinsel and garland, ribbons and bows. With all that glitters during the holidays, it's easy to get so caught up in trying to create a storybook setting for celebration that we forget why we celebrate—or we leave ourselves no time to do it. As you think about all the holiday delights you want to arrange for your friends and family, try to choose just the ones that matter the most. In your choosing, remember that sometimes the most wonderful Christmas memories are those that bear the mark of quiet simplicity.

On that first Christmas night, Jesus was not swaddled in intricately woven cloths, nor did He lay His head on a pillow of satin and velvet. He lay in a simple manger—crudely made and filled with feeding straw. The marks of simplicity—and yet, we remember.

Twenty-Five Ways to Simplify

1. Remember the three "P's" for a peaceful holiday—pray, plan, and prepare.

2. Hold a family meeting early in the year and talk about how you will celebrate. Set a budget and stick to it.

3. Draw names for gift giving and set a limit on how much you will spend.

4. If you buy gifts early in the year, keep a list of what you have purchased and for whom.

5. Make a gift list including sizes and favorite colors. Never go shopping without your list.

6. Remember that babies and young toddlers have no expectations for Christmas. Keep their gifts simple.

7. Give ten percent of what you spend buying gifts to a charity or needy family.

8. Exchange baby-sitting with a friend so you can leave your toddlers safely at home when you go to the mall.

9. Keep all your gift receipts in a separate box or envelope to make returns easier.

10. Decorate just your porch area instead of your entire yard.

11. Exchange decorating help with a friend. Spend one day together at her house and one day at yours.

12. Send cards and letters for New Year's or Valentine's Day instead of for Christmas.

13. Use postcards instead of greeting cards or consider making your own cards with a favorite family photo.

14. Make gift tags from recycled Christmas cards.

15. When entertaining, select a simple menu and use it more than once.

16. Host a potluck dinner and ask your guests to bring side dishes and desserts.

17. When you get together with aging relatives or friends, take time to record a few memories—video, audio, or in writing.

18. Leave a notebook open on the kitchen counter and each day write down some of your blessings. Ask friends and family to participate.

> It is the simple things of life that make living worthwhile.
> —*Laura Ingalls Wilder*

19. With your family, decide on your favorite holiday traditions and let the others go.

20. Mark off times on your December calendar to devote to your family. Decide together how you want to spend this time together.

21. Leave your car at home and stroll through a neighborhood to look at Christmas decorations.

22. Roast marshmallows in the fireplace.

23. Take turns opening gifts so that each gift can be appreciated.

24. After the younger children have opened their gifts, put some of the toys away and bring them out on a rainy day in January.

25. On a Christmas afternoon, bring out a jigsaw puzzle or board game and savor the quiet time.

Late on a sleepy, star-spangled night,
angels peeled back the sky

just like you would tear open
a sparkling Christmas present.

The world had a Savior!

The angels called it, "Good News," and it was.

—LARRY LIBBY

Simple Pleasures

And in all this cold
Decembering—
A gentle time for sweet
remembering.
—*D. Morgan*

The following easy no-bake cookie recipe is a sweet way to remind your children that Jesus was born in a stable and that His very first bed was a manger filled with hay. The "sheep" in the recipe help children think about the shepherds who were taking care of their sheep on a hillside near Bethlehem when the angels appeared to them. After the shepherds heard the "Good News" that a Savior was born, they hurried to the stable to visit the baby Jesus—maybe some of the shepherds carried their littlest lambs with them.

SHEEP IN THE HAY

1 6-ounce package of chocolate or butterscotch morsels
1/2 cup peanut butter
3-ounce can chow mein noodles
2 cups miniature marshmallows

Combine the chocolate or butterscotch morsels with the peanut butter in a bowl and cook on high in the Microwave for 1 minute. Stir the mixture and then microwave for an additional 1–1/2 minutes until it is completely melted. Add chow mein noodles and 1–1/2 cups of the marshmallows to the mixture and toss with two forks as if you were tossing a salad. Drop tablespoons of the mixture onto waxed paper to form haystacks. Ask the children to place the "sheep," (remaining marshmallows) into the haystacks and press. Allow 30 minutes for the cookies to harden on the waxed paper or place in the refrigerator to speed up process. Yield—24 cookies

Treasures of the Heart

> Mary quietly treasured these
> things in her heart
> and thought about them often.
> *Luke 2:19*

Moonlight transforms a light dusting of snow into silver frosting spread on tree branches. But, alas, in the morning, when the warm sun peeks over the mountains, the snow is gone and all that remains is a pleasant memory.

December is the perfect time to start a journal so you can capture the sweet blessings that surround this most precious season of the year. Create a special corner in your home where you can linger for a few moments each day to savor the gifts God has given you. Writing in a journal is one way that you, like Mary the mother of Jesus, can treasure these gifts in your heart.

Reflections

When you find a few moments to slip away to a cozy corner of your house or to the back table of your favorite coffee shop, here are just a few ideas for quiet reflection. Expressing your thoughts on paper is one way to turn a sweet memory into a keepsake of the heart.

> The beauty of the written word is that it can be held close to the heart and read over and over again.
>
> —*Florence Littauer*

- Finding beauty outside my window
- Things that make me smile
- What Christmas means to me
- The people I love
- Memories of Christmas mornings
- Favorite Scripture verses
- Three reasons to be thankful
- A gift to give to Jesus this Christmas
- Traditions that I love
- My favorite Christmas carol
- The best present I ever gave
- The best present I ever received
- Someone I will miss this Christmas
- How I want this Christmas to be remembered
- A love note to Jesus

Scripture Treasures

One way to find room for what really matters during the holidays is to read carefully through the Christmas story as it is told in the Bible. Try to discover a new treasure even if the words are familiar to you.

And while they were there, the time came for her baby to be born. She gave birth to her first child, a son. She wrapped him snugly in strips of cloth and laid him in a manger, because there was no room for them in the village inn.

That night some shepherds were in the fields outside the village, guarding their flocks of sheep. Suddenly, an angel of the Lord appeared among them, and the radiance of the Lord's glory surrounded them. They were terribly frightened, but the angel reassured them.

"Don't be afraid!" he said. "I bring you good news of great joy for everyone! The Savior—yes, the Messiah, the Lord—has been born tonight in Bethlehem, the city of David! And this is how you will recognize him: You will find a baby lying in a manger, wrapped snugly in strips of cloth!"

Suddenly, the angel was joined by a vast host of others—the armies of heaven—praising God: "Glory to God in the highest heaven, and peace on earth to all whom God favors."

When the angels had returned to heaven,
the shepherds said to each other, "Come
on, let's go to Bethlehem! Let's see this
wonderful thing that has happened,
which the Lord has told us about."

Luke 2:6–15

SCRIPTURE TREASURE:

When the angel announced the good news that a Savior was born, Luke 2:13 says that a vast host of angels were praising God. Some Bible scholars believe there were thousands upon thousands of angels. Tonight when it is dark, step outside and look up at the sky and try to imagine what it would be like to hear so many angels singing praises to God.

The star appeared to them, guiding them to Bethlehem. It went ahead of them and stopped over the place where the child was. When they saw the star, they were filled with joy! They entered the house where the child and his mother, Mary, were, and they fell down before him and worshiped him. Then they opened their treasure chests and gave him gifts of gold, frankincense, and myrrh.

Matthew 2:9–11

SCRIPTURE TREASURE:

There is a special meaning behind each of the gifts the Magi brought. Gold was a sought-after treasure—the king of the metals and a most appropriate gift to honor the newborn King. Frankincense was a sacred perfume used by the Jewish priest as an offering of purity. How appropriate to bring it to the One who would always live a pure and holy life. Myrrh was a costly spice used to prepare a body for burial. At first, it seems like an unusual gift to bring a newborn babe. But somehow the Magi understood that the Son of God must exchange the glory of heaven not only for the lowliness of a stable, but also for the humility of a cross.

The meaning of the gifts is this: Gold for the King of Kings. Frankincense for His sinless life. Myrrh for the One who would rather die than live without you in heaven.

Trouble at the Inn

By DINA DONAHUE,
from *GUIDEPOSTS MAGAZINE*

Wally was nine that year and in the second grade, though he should have been in the fourth. Most people in town knew that he had difficulty in keeping up. He was big and clumsy, slow in movement and mind. Still, Wally was well liked by the other children in his class, all of whom were smaller than he, though the boys had trouble hiding their irritation when Wally would ask to play ball with them—or play any game for that matter in which winning was most important.

Most often they would find a way to keep him out, but Wally would hang around anyway—not sulking, just hoping. He was always a helpful boy and a natural protector, paradoxically, of the underdog. Sometimes if the older boys chased the younger ones away, it would always be Wally who'd say, "Can't they stay? They're not bother."

Wally fancied the idea of being a shepherd with a flute in the Christmas pageant that year, but the play's director, Miss Lumbard, assigned him to a more important role. After all, she reasoned, the Innkeeper did not have too many lines, and Wally's size would make his refusal of lodging to Joseph more forceful.

And so it happened that the usual large audience gathered for the town's yearly extravaganza of crèches, beards, crowns, halos and a whole stage full of squeaky voices. No one on stage or off was more caught up in the magic of the night than Wallace Purling. They said later that he stood in the wings and watched the performance with such fascination that from time to time Miss Lumbard had to make sure he didn't wander on-stage before his cue.

Then the time came when Joseph appeared, slowly, tenderly guiding Mary to the door of the inn. Joseph knocked hard on the wooden door set into the painted backdrop. Wally the Innkeeper was there, waiting.

"What do you want?" demanded Wally, swinging the door open with a brusque gesture.

"We seek lodging."

"Seek it elsewhere." Wally looked straight ahead but spoke vigorously. "The inn is filled."

"Sir, we have asked everywhere in vain. We have traveled far and are very weary."

"There is no room in this inn for you." Wally looked properly stern.

"Please, good innkeeper, this is my wife, Mary. She is heavy with child and needs a place to rest. Surely you must have some small corner for her. She is so tired."

Now, for the first time, the Innkeeper relaxed his stiff stance and looked down at Mary. With that, there was a long pause, long enough to make the audience a bit tense with embarrassment.

"No! Be gone!" the prompter whispered from the wings.

117

"No!" Wally repeated automatically. "Be gone!"

Joseph placed his arm around Mary and Mary laid her head upon her husband's shoulder and the two of them started to move away. The Innkeeper did not return inside his inn, however. Wally stood there in the doorway, watching the forlorn couple. His mouth was open, his brow creased with concern, his eyes filling unmistakably with tears.

And suddenly this Christmas pageant became different from all others.

"Don't go, Joseph," Wally called out. "Bring Mary back." And Wallace Purling's face grew into a bright smile. "You can have my room."

Is There Room in My Heart?

More than two thousand years ago Joseph and Mary knocked at the door of an overcrowded inn and were told, "No room." Today, Jesus knocks softly at the door of our overcrowded hearts. With all the excitement and joy of making this a Christmas to remember, let us promise ourselves to find room for the One whose birth we celebrate.

~

Thanks be to God for his unspeakable Gift—

indescribable

inestimable

incomparable

inexpressibly precious beyond words.

—LOIS LEBAR

ACKNOWLEDGMENTS

"Candle of Hope" by John Fischer, from Daily Devotional, Purpose Driven Life, www.purposedrivenlife.com, December 24, 2004. Used by permission.

"Especially at Christmas" by Celestine Sibley, from Christmas in Georgia, Peachtree Publishers, Ltd., Atlanta, Georgia, ©1985. Used by permission.

"The Real Treasure" by Judy Gordon, ©2005. Used by permission of the author.

"Mary's Song" by Luci Shaw, from Polishing the Petoskey Stone, Harold Shaw Publishers, ©1990. Used by permission of the author.

"Hailey's Gift" by Megan Chrane, ©2005. Used by permission of the author.

"Trouble at the Inn" by Dina Donohue, reprinted with permission from Guideposts magazine, copyright © 1966 by Guideposts, Carmel, NY 10512. All rights reserved.

Untitled traditions:

Tradition about the Easy Bake Oven by Laura Burkett. ©2005. Used by permission of the author.

Tradition about wrapping presents for Jesus by Danae Jacobson, ©2005. Used by permission of the author.